Anonymous

Obituary Addresses and Proceedings of the Bar,

on the occasion of the death of Abraham O. Zabriskie, LL. D., late

chancellor of the state of New Jersey

Anonymous

Obituary Addresses and Proceedings of the Bar,
*on the occasion of the death of Abraham O. Zabriskie, LL. D., late chancellor of the
state of New Jersey*

ISBN/EAN: 9783337403393

Printed in Europe, USA, Canada, Australia, Japan

Cover: Foto ©ninafisch / pixelio.de

More available books at **www.hansebooks.com**

Anonymous

Obituary Addresses and Proceedings of the Bar,
on the occasion of the death of Abraham O. Zabriskie, LL. D., late chancellor of the state of New Jersey

ISBN/EAN: 9783337403393

Printed in Europe, USA, Canada, Australia, Japan

Cover: Foto ©ninafisch / pixelio.de

More available books at **www.hansebooks.com**

Obituary Addresses

AND

PROCEEDINGS OF THE BAR

On the Occasion of the Death of

ABRAHAM O. ZABRISKIE, LL.D.,

Late Chancellor of the State of New Jersey.

PRINTED FOR THE HUDSON COUNTY BAR.

JERSEY CITY:
PRINTED BY JOHN H. LYON,
—1874—

PROCEEDINGS OF THE HUDSON COUNTY BAR.

——◆——

Proceedings of the meeting of the Bar of Hudson county, held in the Common Council Chamber, at the City Hall, in Jersey City, on Monday, the 7th day of June, 1873, to take suitable action upon the death of the late Chancellor Abraham O. Zabriskie.

The Honorable Joseph D. Bedle was called to the chair, and Isaac Romaine was appointed secretary.

REMARKS BY JUDGE BEDLE.

The death of Chancellor Zabriskie, so sudden and unexpected, almost shocks us to silence. A few weeks ago he left his home, just freed from the cares of a great office, apparently buoyant with health and giving promise of a ripe old age, and to-day we meet to mourn his loss and bear him to the tomb. The event has cast a deep gloom over this community. Here he lived for years, here he attained his greatest successes, and here, amongst his professional brethren and friends, will he

be mostly missed. His loss, however, is not confined
to us immediately, for his learning, ability and personal
worth were acknowledged and appreciated throughout
and beyond the State. I well remember the night of
his departure upon his fatal journey. To him, it was
the entrance upon a series of observations and enjoy-
ments, which would be a fitting change and relief from
the labors of his judicial career, and when ended, would
result in renewed vigor and preparation for further
usefulness and duty. He felt, as could be readily told
from his conversation, that he was fully able physically
to meet all the toil and exigencies of the trip. He
succeeded in crossing the continent, but on his return,
while tarrying at Truckee, a little village upon the
Sierra Nevada, he fell a victim to disease, and most
unexpectedly died. He intended, as I am informed,
to reach home in life, the very day his body was
brought thither by his faithful friend Mr. Knapp.
We meet now in the deep solemnity of the occasion,
to pay a last tribute to his memory and to give expression to our grief.

Chancellor Zabriskie was a most remarkable man,
both in physical appearance and in intrinsic mental
strength. Those who saw him for the first, knew
at once that he was no ordinary man, and those who

were familiar with him, and especially those who experienced the weight of his power as a professional antagonist, well understood that it was great and formidable. He was a thoroughly read lawyer, and while at the bar, excelled in the science of the common law. His mind was eminently practical, and could easily adapt itself to the plainest comprehensions. In this was one of the secrets of his success as an advocate. He was fertile in analogies, and used the plainest facts and principles of every day life with wonderful facility, to illustrate his arguments. In this he had no equal at the bar. That quality was always felt before a jury, and frequently was dangerously effective against an adversary before educated minds. Though possessing that faculty in so high a degree, he was always profound and learned in a purely legal argument. His research was careful and courts were always aided by the results of his labor and reflection. I heard an eminent judge, who for years adorned the bench of the Court of Errors and Appeals of this State, and whose just judgment of men all will concede, say that Mr. Zabriskie had no superior in strength before that court.

As a chancellor, he served the State with faithfulness, and promptly, ably and satisfactorily performed the duties of the office. His judicial record will always be regarded as a very valuable part of our jurisprudence.

As presiding officer of the Court of Errors and Appeals, he was dignified, yet genial, and in the labors and conferences of that court I have seen some of the most striking evidences of his learning and fertility of thought.

As a neighbor and friend I shall miss him very much. He had social qualities of a high order—cultivated, rational and refined. To those who knew little of him, his appearance might not always indicate how good a heart he possessed, but all who partook of his hospitality or saw much of his daily life, knew that he was companionable, considerate and kind to others, in a high degree.

To his great abilities was added great industry, and these, with his integrity, which was undoubted, enabled him under Providence to rise to the summit of his profession, and now, after having served the State in its highest judicial office with honor and usefulness, and while his vigor was unimpaired, and death apparently remote, he is taken from us most unexpectedly, leaving by that very fact the prominence of his character more distinct, and the force of his example the greater. Such men are a serious loss to us all. For life at best is but short to acquire a profound knowledge of the law, and when obtained, accompanied with the fruits of experience and a ripe judgment, the benefit is not alone to the individual, but to the public at large. His example is a bright legacy to the profession, and the qualities that made him great should be noted and imitated.

On motion, the chair appointed the following Committee on Resolutions: ABRAHAM S. JACKSON, ISAAC W. SCUDDER, PETER BENTLEY, JACOB WEART, WASHINGTON B. WILLIAMS.

The committee retired and reported the following resolutions, which were unanimously adopted:

Resolved, By the death of CHANCELLOR ZABRISKIE, New Jersey has lost one of her most eminent citizens.

He was possessed of a mind stored with useful, practical and scientific knowledge, which rendered his services of great value in those enterprises of public improvement which has marked the character and attended the progress of our country. His judgment was sound and his sagacity far-reaching, and, as a man, familiar with general affairs, he achieved a distinguished reputation.

As an *Advocate,* possessed of a facility of illustration, an untiring energy and great scope of mind, he was among the most powerful men of his time.

As a *Lawyer*, he was among the most learned; with the ability to apply, with great effect, his varied acquirements, in the causes in which he was engaged.

As *Surrogate* and *Prosecutor of the Pleas* of the County of Bergen, he evinced a care, industry and ability, which gave evidence of his fitness for those important positions.

As a *Member* of the Legislative Department of the Government, he left his impress on the laws of our State, many of our important statutes having been framed by him and passed at his suggestion.

He performed the arduous duties of *Chancellor* of the State with a promptness, energy and ability which challenged the admiration and won the respect and confidence of the profession and the public.

The *State Constitutional Convention*, over whose deliberations he had been called to preside, had formed the highest expectations from his mature judgment and large experience, and will greatly miss him in their deliberations.

As a *Man*, he was kind, generous and benevolent. He cultivated with success those social virtues, which shed a charming influence upon society, and in his friendships, he was sincere and devoted.

We, his associates, looked forward with the expectation that our departed *Friend* would have enjoyed an old age of usefulness and repose, shedding around his declining years, those mellowed rays, which would attract by their charm and soothe by their mildness; but in this we have been disappointed. Our memory of his eminence will be his monument, and our grief the tribute to his loss.

Resolved, That we sincerely condole with the members of his family, at their sudden bereavement, and tender to them our heartfelt sympathy.

Resolved, That the Secretary of this meeting transmit a copy of these resolutions to his family, and cause the same to be published in the daily newspapers, and that the courts of the County of Hudson be requested to enter the same on their minutes.

REMARKS ON RESOLUTIONS.

REMARKS BY MR. JACOB WEART.

Mr. Chairman—But a few days ago, we bore to the tomb the remains of our lamented friend, the Hon. Joseph F. Randolph, and before the year had completed the first half of its cycle, the sad announcement fell upon our ears that the late Chancellor was no more; and the bar is again convened, by that messenger who comes so unexpectedly, and at an hour that we know not of, to call us hence. To the departed, death came without a warning, his sickness was very short, and he passed out of the world unconscious that his end was approaching. And we are assembled to express our sentiments upon his worth as a man, to extend our sympathies to his bereaved family, and to put upon record a parting word of the loss which has fallen to our profession.

When I came to Jersey City in 1852, a friendless

stranger in this city, I soon found in Mr. Zabriskie a
warm personal friend; he was very kind to me, he in-
vited me into his family circle, he assisted me in every
way he could professionally, his extensive law library
was always open to me, and in this way we became
strong personal friends. I was a great admirer of his
profound learning and ability as a lawyer; and his
fame as a counsellor and advocate had became a household word to the bar and people of the State, as will
be seen by a short reference to our political history.

In the year 1859, His Excellency, William A.
Newell, selected Mr. Zabriskie as his first choice for
Chancellor, and nominated him to the Senate, and the
Senate being politically opposed to the Governor de-
clined to confirm the nomination, and the memorable
struggle was entered into, which left the State for a
year without a Chancellor.

At the ensuing election, His Excellency, Charles S.
Olden was elected Governor, but the Senate remained
politically opposed to him. I remember to have
visited Governor Olden, at Princeton, to present the
name of Mr. Zabriskie for the office of Chancellor, and
after the legislature convened, Governor Olden advised me that he would nominate Mr. Zabriskie as
Chancellor, provided he could be confirmed, but if he

could not be confirmed, he thought the interests of the
State required that his name should not be sent in, but
another nomination made; and he gave Mr. Zabriskie's
friends time to see if the confirmation could be secured;
but the memory of the struggle of the year previous
was too fresh and bitter to allow of his confirmation.
When His Excellency Marcus L. Ward was elected in
1865, and it became known that the office of Chancellor would become vacant, the bar of the State generally
looked to Mr. Zabriskie as the coming man, and he was
accordingly nominated and confirmed. I mention
these facts to show what a strong hold he had upon
the public confidence, having been the first choice for
the office of Chancellor of three successive Republican
Governors.

Our chairman having spoken of him as a Chancellor, I desire to call attention to a few other remarkable
traits of his character. Mr. Zabriskie was a lawyer
and not a politician, yet he took a deep interest in all
of the affairs of State, and the crowning act of his life
was his opposition and defeat of the extension of the
monopoly grants to the Camden and Amboy Railroad
Company.

I attended the great public meeting at Park Hall,
in this city, where he was the chief public speaker,

and his power and eloquence on that occasion was so great, that he fairly thrilled his audience as it were by an electric shock ; he repeated his speech before a committee of the legislature at Trenton, and the extension of the monopoly was dead. Great as Mr. Zabriskie's services were in the two highest courts of the State where he presided, in my judgment they fall infinitely short of his great struggle for the rights of the people of the State in his successful effort to defeat the extension of the monopoly privilege, and the result is, that to-day we have a free railroad law; without his aid, we would most likely still have remained under the monopoly power, and would have so continued until 1889.

Before I close I would like to add a tribute to him as a student for the benefit of the young. Mr. Zabriskie started out in life with the design of acquiring knowledge and making himself useful in his day and generation. He told me that although his father resided within twelve miles of Princeton college, and that he kept horses and servants, so that he could have sent for him at any time, yet when he went to Princeton, at the opening of the session, he remained there until the session closed, as he did not wish to have his course of study broken in upon by journeys to visit his parents and friends.

Mr. Zabriskie never got above the books, and always consulted authorities. I was struck with this on one occasion. I went to employ him as counsel in an important matter, and after a short consultation about the case, he suggested that we turn to the books; he said, I always like to consult authority and be guided by established principles and decisions.

He was a warm personal friend, I ever found him so through life, but he has gone. He passed away distant, from his home, and amid strangers, upon the western slopes of the Pacific; he was however full of years, full of honors, he had earned a fame which will go down to posterity as long as reports are read, and the law is honored; and the last tribute that that we can offer, is a tear by the side of his bier.

REMARKS BY HON. CHARLES H. WINFIELD.

Mr. Chairman—I cannot let this occasion pass without bearing testimony to the worth of my former teacher, guide and friend. No man, said the great philosopher, can be considered great until he is dead; but those who best knew Chancellor Zabriskie will admit

that it did not need death, in whose awful presence envy
and all the baser passions of the soul are still, to issue
the patent of his nobility. He was, while yet among
us, in himself and of himself, every inch a king; not
from fortuitous circumstances, but from making himself
an embodiment of the truth of the Roman maxim,
quisque suœ fortunœ faber.

Three years as a student under him, and part of that
time at a table in his private office inspired me with a
high appreciation of his legal acquirements, and his
sterling qualities as a man. At that time he represented
this county in the State Senate, the only political office,
I believe, he ever held. Twelve years afterward, when
I had the honor to represent this county in the same
body, an incident occurred which it is now permissible
to make public, inasmuch as he whom it most concerned
is no more. The remarks of Mr. Weart have brought
it to my recollection. Pardon the reference which a
recital of the incident makes to myself:

Just previous to his nomination to the office of Chancellor, and while those in the opposite political party
knew nothing of the Governor's plans, or that Mr.
Zabriskie's name was to be presented, he and I were
walking from the depot to our hotel in Trenton, when
he asked me if I had any objection to his being nomi-

nated to the Chancellorship; at the same time remarking that he was getting somewhat advanced in years and would like to close his professional life with that honorable position. Without hesitation the assurance was readily given that, I not only had no objection, but would gladly assist in furthering his wishes. To understand the point of his inquiry, it may be proper to observe that, at that time the Senate was composed of eleven Republicans and ten Democrats. Mr. Zabriskie, by his manly course upon certain railroad questions, a few years previously, had become obnoxious to a particular corporation which then held no inconsiderable control in the State. At least one Senator on the Republican side was of that corporation. A few days afterward Mr. Zabriskie's nomination was sent in by the Governor. Combinations were immediately made for his rejection in the Senate. The Democrats acting as a unit, with the assistance of one Republican, were sufficient for that purpose, and that assistance was assured. A caucus was called to complete the plans. The ten of the opposition were there. Among them were grey-headed men, men of ability and experience. Views were expressed, and they were adverse to the confirmation. Being the youngest and least experienced of the body, my opinion was last called for. It was freely given. How could they ask me to do such a great wrong to the man who had guided my footsteps to an honorable profession, who had given me his friendship when a poor, friendless boy, and how could I, now that the opportunity was at hand withhold my gratitude. I was sorry to differ from my friends, but honor compelled me to vote for his confirmation and a caucus had no right to decree otherwise. If it insisted upon such right I must ask leave to withdraw. Much to their credit, several Senators approved of my course and we were all left free to vote as we pleased. Thus the opposition was disorganized and the nominee's confirmation assured. To me the result was profoundly gratifying, and the privilege of doing what I did remains one of the pleasures of memory. He died without knowing the history of that struggle.

How often since his death have I recalled his wish to close his professional life with the high office he so ably filled. It has turned out to be more real than either of us thought. But a few days intervened between the laying aside of his official robes and his death. But a few days ago we appeared before him, the judge ; to-day, upon his coffin we mingle our tears. He stepped from the bench to the tomb ; he filled his term of office and died. Thus he lives in our memory as a *Chancellor* meeting in full the judicial requirements of Lord Bacon, rather learned, than witty; venerable, than plausible; and more advised, than confident.

COMMUNICATION FROM MR. W. B. WILLIAMS.

Mr. A. S. Jackson stated that he had received from Mr. Williams, who was unavoidably absent, a few written remarks, with the sentiments of which he fully concurred, and which he would ask leave to read, as follows :

One of the most prominent figures which I recall in looking back to the beginning of my professional life, is that of Mr. Zabriskie. There were giants in those days at the New Jersey bar, both in body and mind. Mr. Asa Whitehead, Gov. Pennington, Mr. Whelpley, Mr. Dayton, Chief-Justice Green and others, then in full vigor, were all men of commanding presence as well as of powerful intellect. We students used to look up to their tall, dignified forms, so different from our own and from the men of to day, and which united

with courtly manners and with distinguished skill and
eloquence to fill out the ideal of the leading lawyer.
Mr. Zabriskie was their peer—and as early as I can
remember was among the foremost. In Bergen county
he had held almost absolute sway over juries, and it
did not take him long to show that he was worthy of
the utmost attention and confidence from our own
citizens.

His manner in court I remember with much pleasure.
He would often commence his address in a low tone,
scarcely audible, and with apparent embarrassment.
Then he would place one foot on a chair, and leaning
confidentially toward the jury, would attract their
attention by that wonderful illustration of the horse,
which he could somehow apply to every case as aptly
as ever an anecdote of Mr. Lincoln's fitted its object.
And soon he would glide into a copious flow of statement and illustration supplied from his keen memory
of the testimony, and ingenious analogies, emphasized
often by the weight of his own assertion or opinion,
and sometimes rising into the plane of eloquence.
His strong points, however, were his clear and homely
way of putting the case to the jury, coupled with
untiring patience and Protean ingenuity in presenting
the law to the court.

In the office he was a most valuable adviser. His apprehension was as quick as the statement; he was familiar with decided cases, and with principles, and his strong practical sense showed him almost intuitively how they would apply. His perception of character was keen; he was eminently a man fitted for active life, not a literary man or a book-worm, though his fine library attested his taste and love for books. His manner and bearing added great weight to what he said in consultation, and he was both by his physical and mental characteristics decided and positive in his views. Yet he was not opinionated. When, as must often happen even to the wisest, further discussion or reflection indicated that he was mistaken, no man was more ready to admit the error and correct it.

To some degree he paid the debt every good lawyer owes to his profession, for he was the law reporter from 1847 to 1853, and his reports are without doubt the best we have had in this State. They set forth in general, a clear statement of the case, and important arguments of counsel; and their head-notes are, so far as I know, unexceptionable. Besides, it so happened that during that period the Supreme Court discussed many interesting and important legal rules. Local and special legislation had not then attained such evil frequency and confusing diversity as now, when they overwhelm the court with dry and uninstructive controversy, and follow us like the frogs of Egypt into our towns, our streets, our sewers, our local administration, and almost our bed-chambers.

The worthy aim of a lawyer's ambition, a dignified post in the administration of public justice, where his hard-earned knowledge and experience can be of the greatest service in maintaining right and redressing wrong, was attained by Mr. Zabriskie, as a fitting close to his honorable career. I will not speak of any particular cases he decided, nor of his judicial qualities, as others of greater experience will do this.

But I would remind you of the patience and attention with which he listened, while Chancellor, to the crude arguments of junior counsel; and explained to them the practice of the court, which he like his learned predecessor, labored to make efficacious and uniform. The rules of court and many decisions testify to the pains he took in this direction.

But what is far more and nobler than kind attention, or forbearance, or practical skill, he loved justice as it should be loved—not because it is on the whole the best policy in human affairs, but for its own sake, for its inherent beauty and fitness, and as the noblest attribute of either man or God. And he sought to administer it, not like a calculating machine or a logic mill, but as a man with the feelings of humanity, to whom nothing human was foreign, who could know and sympathize with human passions and impulses; who could feel affectionate pity for oppressed innocence, hatred of fraud, and holy anger against bold and unblushing guilt.

With these convictions, I am full of sorrow that he has so soon passed away. I could have wished him to remain in his ripening old age to adorn the bench or the Senate; or if in this day of base rotation that were too much to ask, then that he might have walked before us slowly down the vale of years, the Nestor of our bar. But all this is cut off: and we have suffered a loss which we can only submit to, and which it is useless to bewail. The death of a good and great man leaves his good example cleared of his defects or weaknesses, for us to follow. We have a right too, to believe, that such noble and masterful faculties as his, are not to be forever laid away in inaction or obscurity; but that they will be brought out by the Lord of all worlds to be put to some great and worthy purpose, in those vast unknown regions which are full of all past humanity, and whither we also are bound.

REMARKS BY MR. ISAAC S. TAYLOR.

Mr. Chairman—The sorrow that is felt and has been so unmistakeably evinced, to-day, by those of his professional brethren to whom through the association of many years, Chancellor Zabriskie had endeared himself, is I know fully shared by many who have but recently entered upon their legal career, and whose attachments to the deceased were formed in later years. And we, young members of the bar, have just cause for grief, in that one who was ever ready to assist us by valuable counsel, and to encourage us by cheering words, has been suddenly claimed and stricken down by death.

Especially do I—but a very few years since his pupil in the law—desire to add at this time a slight, but a heartfelt, tribute to his memory. And in so doing I am confident that I shall speak the sentiments of all who have been privileged to call him their instructor.

It is not always—nor indeed very often—that the preceptor acquires and retains a large and warm place in the esteem of the pupil. And many an instructor, in terminating his peculiar relation with his scholar, closes the latter's heart to affectionate remembrances of him.

Particularly in a profession where the instruction of others is but incidental to other duties, it would not be surprising if amid the press of business, and constant wear of mind and energy, the lessons taught should be instilled with no accompaniment which in after years would render the method of tuition a pleasure of memory.·

But I am sure that to-day, though saddened as we are by the thought that he is no more, there is nothing but pleasure and love in the breasts of his students as they recall the days and years passed under the tutelage of Mr. Zabriskie.

His careful work in establishing the principles of the law in their minds—his willing explanations of what was hard to be understood—the wonderfully varied practical methods of illustration whereby he made what were apparently the most obscure and difficult matters perfectly intelligible to those under his charge—and in short, his zealous and faithful attention to their instruction cannot be forgotten by them, or remembered with aught but happiness and thankfulness.

He not only impressed their minds with a sense

of his own deep researches in, and thorough mastery of his profession, but produced in them an *interest* in the object of their study, which under his guidance could not lessen or grow cold.

He was as conscientious, and as ready to exert the powers of his practical mind, in the discharge of his duties to those whom he was instructing, as in the fulfillment of his obligations to his clients—and there was no faithlessness towards *them*.

To these characteristics he added the constant exhibition of kindness, consideration and sociability, and thus secured the respect and love of those about him.

His students were always welcome to his home. His general, as well as his law library was at their disposal, and they were made to realize his interest in them. Nor did this interest cease when their formal relations to each other were at an end. Counsel was as freely and fully given—assistance as generously bestowed, and the same genial, social qualities as constantly evinced through succeeding years.

It is not for me to refer to his course at the bar and on the bench, or in the various positions of trust and confidence in which he was so frequently placed —but I have spoken of him as he was known and

loved of me. And now, realizing the fact that he
has gone, there shall remain in calling him to mind
only thoughts fragrant with gratitude, and memories
of respect and honor.

On motion of Mr. Weart it was ordered that the chair be
requested to pronounce, or appoint some person to pronounce
a eulogy on the life and character of the late Chancellor,
at the opening of the October Term of the Hudson County
Circuit Court.

Owing to Judge Bedle's constant engagements in Court,
he was prevented from preparing the eulogy himself, but
appointed the Hon. Isaac W. Scudder to pronounce the
same.

PROCEEDINGS AT THE COURT HOUSE,

———— ◆ ————

REMARKS BY MR. JACOB WEART.

May it please the Court—It becomes my painful duty to announce to the court, that since the last regular term, our late lamented friend, Chancellor Zabriskie, has passed away. For many years he was the leading lawyer of this county, and we looked to him as the Nestor of the bar—he participated in all the struggles of this people, and was their counsellor in public and private affairs; from the scenes of his labors here, he was asked by the State to come up higher, and was made Chancellor. It is fit and proper that when one so distinguished in public and private station passes away, that we pause for a while, and lay aside our business and cares, and direct our thoughts to the memory of the dead.

The bar has taken suitable action in relation to

their bereavement, and at a meeting held in the Common Council Chamber, on the seventh day of July last, a series of resolutions were unanimously adopted, which it affords me great pleasure to now read and present to the court; and at that meeting a person was selected to prepare and pronounce a suitable eulogy upon his life and character at the opening of the term this day.

I would therefore move, your honor, that the resolutions be entered upon the minutes of the court, and that the court do now adjourn.

— —

REMARKS BY JUDGE BEDLE.

The resolutions read, are a truthful and fitting tribute to the memory of Chancellor Zabriskie. It is just that this court should make a record of the death of so distinguished a judge, and a lawyer so learned and able. It is ordered that the resolutions be entered at large upon the minutes, and also that out of respect to the memory of the deceased, the court do now adjourn.

On motion, a meeting of the bar was organized.

Judge Bedle was called to take the chair, and Mr. Jonathan Dixon was appointed secretary.

The chair announced that the Hon. Isaac W. Scudder had been selected, as provided by a previous resolution, to pronounce the eulogy.

Mr. Scudder then pronounced the eulogy.

After the eulogy had been pronounced, it was moved that the chair appoint a committee of five to request a copy of the eulogy for publication, and that the committee prepare and publish for the use of the bar, the eulogy, resolutions, remarks made at the bar meeting, held at the City Hall, and such other matter as they may deem advisable.

The chair appointed Messrs. Weart, Dixon, Williams, Gilchrist, and Ransom such committee.

CORRESPONDENCE.

JERSEY CITY, OCTOBER 8, 1873.

HON. ISAAC W. SCUDDER:

Dear Sir—The bar of this county desire to express their deep sense of gratitude for the eulogy pronounced by you upon the character, life and public services of the late lamented Chancellor Abraham O. Zabriskie.

At a meeting of the bar, a resolution was unanimously passed requesting that you furnish a copy for publication, and we the undersigned, were appointed a committee to solicit from you a copy, and to publish the same. Hoping that you will comply with the request, we remain with great respect,

Yours, very truly,

JACOB WEART,
JONATHAN DIXON,
W. B. WILLIAMS,
ROBERT GILCHRIST,
S. B. RANSOM,

Committee.

JERSEY CITY, OCTOBER 15, 1873.

JACOB WEART, ESQ., CHAIRMAN:

Dear Sir —At your request I place in your hands the address made by me at the opening of the court in Hudson county, at the present October term, on the occasion of the announcement of the death of our friend and neighbor, Chancellor Zabriskie, whose loss caused us so much grief. I regret that the short time in which it was prepared did not afford sufficient opportunity to do justice to a man, who was so highly appreciated by us, as a judge, a friend and a citizen.

Yours truly,

I. W. SCUDDER.

ADDRESS BY HON. ISAAC W. SCUDDER.

It is well that there are periods in the history of men when they are willing to forget their jealousies and rivalries, and with a common sentiment and united voice, both feel and express their appreciation for and admiration of those who by labor and good conduct have achieved eminence and distinction. We bestow praise upon the artist who with great skill groups and combines on the canvass scenes from nature or history; we dwell with pleasure on the animated narrative of the historian; the genius of the poet kindles our enthusiasm; deeds in arms excite our love of the heroic; and we follow the grand discoveries of men of science, wondering at the extent to which they can penetrate the laws of the universe, and the facility with which they can apply them to the advancement of mankind. The statesman, though he may be covered with obloquy in his time, has the appreciation of succeeding generations. The eminence which is achieved by the professional man, it too frequently happens, lives only in the memory of his cotemporaries, and the historian is scarcely alive to the consciousness of his existence. Yet while this is so, the discipline, the protracted labor, the abstraction of mind, and the great struggle which gives distinction to the lawyer of rank and eminence, would in some other pursuits win a degree of fame which would be transmitted to many generations. How much of patience, of labor, of tact, of endurance, and even of heroic effort, is oftentimes displayed in the life of the lawyer, which if evinced by the soldier, the statesman, the man of science, or letters, would win an enduring fame.

But let us pass from generalities to particulars. One from among us, familiar to us by the intercourse of every day life, distinguished as a lawyer and a judge, has departed, and we are called upon on this occasion to express our appreciation of his merits and his character.

The family of Mr. Zabriskie was well known in New Jersey, and this is not the occasion for a biography, but for the expression of our views of his life and character as a man, a lawyer and a judge. Like the sturdy oak, he was somewhat slow of growth; no precocious brilliancy, no showy flowers of a short season marked his development. Amid a quiet, slow, agricultural people, who held on to the traditions of the past, rather than courted the developments of the future, he grew to the maturity of his intellectual powers, and in the county of Bergen he gathered strength which lasted during his life. In this, how great was his advantage! The man who at an early age is thrown amid the stir, excitement and strife of the city, even though careful not to waste his powers, is apt to be forced to a too rapid growth. Early brilliancy and energetic effort, stimulated by surrounding influences, oftentimes pass away before the meridian of life has been reached. At Hackensack, Mr. Zabriskie had time to lay broad and deep the foundation for the superstructure which was afterwards erected. Among the people of Bergen county, slow to give their confidence, but which when once given is lasting, Mr. Zabriskie won a degree of consideration which probably they have never bestowed more fully on any other man.

In the year 1838 he was appointed Surrogate of the County of Bergen, and was reappointed to that office, which he held for ten years. But he was not content simply to learn the accurate statement of the accounts of executors and administrators, (and in this particular, the records of his office show that he was not excelled), but he acquired a knowledge of the history of ecclesiastical law as pertaining to the estates of decedents, which made his counsels valuable at subsequent periods of his life. In the administration of that office, he evinced a method and accuracy which distinguished his life; and the discipline and care about minute details here acquired lasted him ever afterwards; and there was no man in the profession, in litigated causes in the Orphans' Court or Prerogative Court, whose services were more valuable than his. One of his associates in the profession, who, after he had left Hackensack, called him in to aid in a difficult cause in the Orphans' Court of one of our inland counties, the preparation of which had not originally been made by Mr. Zabriskie, said of him, that he readily mastered every detail of an intricate transaction, and argued the cause as if every witness had been before him, and every minute particular had been familiar to him. To use his expression, the dead manuscript on which the testimony was written, seemed to be alive.

This illustrates in the man of intellectual power, the value of the discipline acquired by what is sometimes called useless drugery.

In 1842, Mr. Zabriskie was appointed Prosecutor of the Pleas of the County of Bergen, an office which among the . order-loving and law-enforcing

people of New Jersey has seldom been bestowed
on the unworthy. In this office he became master
of the principles of the criminal law, and though
aided by that strong sense of justice which always
characterized the descendants of the Hollanders, no
man in that county, amenable to the criminal law,
went unpunished for lack of effort on his part. On
account of the ability thus displayed, he was called
upon frequently afterwards, both to prosecute and
defend in criminal causes. He was reappointed to
this office, and if I mistake not, before the expiration
of his second term, he removed to Jersey City. In
an agricultural county such as Bergen then was, Mr.
Zabriskie was frequently called on to prosecute or
defend civil causes, in which the title to land was
involved. In this way he either became experienced
as a practical surveyor, or developed that knowledge
as a mathematician and a man of figures, which he had
acquired, and which he took pleasure in exercising.
He was familiar with the proprietary history of New
Jersey, and he understood every patent in the old
Field Book of Bergen county, and the common lands
assigned to each patent. So much had this taste been
cultivated, that after he became Chancellor, he had a
copy of some portion of this ancient and valuable

record hung up in his office, where it was ready for inspection. The reported cases in which he was engaged showed how thoroughly he was a land-lawyer ; and every member of the bar, in cases where the title to land was involved, felt how formidable Mr. Z. was as an adversary, and how much confidence and strength he acquired by his assistance. Samuel Berry—the old surveyor of Hackensack, who knew every tract of land from the Bergen line to the Kills, and by whom occupied, said to me, that Mr. Zabriskie was the most useful counsel in a land cause, that he knew. He thus acquired habits of patience and labor, so that tedious details, from which many able and brilliant men would turn away with aversion, became to him matters of pleasure, so long as the pursuit proved useful.

Before he left Hackensack, in 1849, he had so impressed the Supreme Court by his thorough research, and his capacity for patient labor, that he was made reporter of that tribunal, and held that position until some time in the year 1855.

He thus acquired a fondness for the pursuits of his profession, so much so, that I once heard a Hackensack lawyer, younger than Mr. Zabriskie, say of him, that in those days he took as much pleasure in the investigation and trial of a cause, as he did in eating his breakfast. Thus disciplined, with his armor well made and accurately fitted, he sought a wider field for the display of his powers, when in 1849 he came to the county of Hudson to reside.

When Mr. Zabriskie made his residence in the county of Hudson, he was no stranger among our people. The county of Hudson was set off from the county of Bergen in the year 1840. Hackensack, previous to 1840, was the county seat. Jurymen from the old township of Bergen, now Hudson county, assembled four times a year at Hackensack. These jurymen knew Mr. Zabriskie as a prominent lawyer who was engaged in every cause of importance in the county. Every man who proved a will, or administered on an estate came in personal contact with him. Political associations, which exert a large influence in our country, in agricultural districts, made the inhabitants from the New Jersey state line to Kill Von Kull somewhat acquainted with each other. The people of old Powles' Hook fought their political battles at a place located on the road to Hackensack, where the Three Pigeons, perched on the top of the tavern sign, looked down on the combat with the utmost complacency, without fluttering a wing or winking an eye.

One of the results of this association of people was, that when Mr. Zabriskie came to reside among us, having been to some extent a leader in politics in Bergen county, he was taken up by the people of Hudson county and elected to the State Senate in the year 1850, and served for three years in that important post. His term of service included the years 1851, 1852 and 1853. Here he took an important part in legislation, and thus came in personal contact with many leading men in the State of New Jersey, which resulted greatly to his advantage in after years.

He also took some part as one of the committee of citizens who framed the voluminous charter for Jersey City, which was passed March 18, 1851, some of the provisions of which were drafted by him.

His hand can be seen in many acts of the legislature which were passed while he was in the Senate.

I will refer to two important bills drafted by him, and which became laws.

The legislative enactments of a government are the monuments, which to a great extent guide the historian in tracing the progress of any people. The wants and necessities, as well as the passions and prejudices of a nation are largely portrayed in the statute book. The movement to abolish imprisonment for debt had its strongest impulse in the territory comprised in the county of Hudson. Situated opposite the city of New York, we caught the impulse which moved the people of the great metropolis, and determined that the passenger who crossed our borders should no longer dread the Hackensack jail and its formidable keeper. Imprisonment for debt was abolished in the year 1840, and subsequently its perpetual prohibition was declared by the Constitution of 1844.

As a result new remedies were sought for. The man who furnished materials, or bestowed his labor in the erection of houses, desired to have a lien on that which his property or his industry created. The cautious lawyers, who held the doctrine, that a contract could not be binding unless by the consent of the party contracting, resisted the notion that there could be a lien on a building erected, except with the consent of the owner. The new order of things arising to some extent from the abolition of imprisonment for debt, led to the adoption of a new remedy, and the law of lien, derived so largely from the civil law, arose in importance. Lien laws, as applicable to the erection of houses, were from time to time passed by the legislature, which were crude and badly digested, and which had only an application to certain districts in the State.

Some of our ablest and most learned lawyers declared that these laws could not be carried into effect. Mr. Zabriskie, however, saw the tendency of the times, and with practical good sense and judgment, embodied the laws in a compact and working system, which has remained without serious alteration, and he so framed it, that whilst it afforded proper protection to the material-man and the laborer, the capitalist and the man who desired to erect his own dwelling had a way pointed out, by which they could have sufficient freedom to carry on their enterprises.

Representing a county bounding on one of the noblest rivers and greatest harbors on the continent, destined to become great in the history of the nation by reason of its proximity to the commercial metropolis of this western empire, he became convinced that his constituents should have the benefit of that rule of the local common law of the State of New Jersey, which held that the shore owner could dock

out in front of his land below high water mark, so
far as might be proper or necessary for commercial
purposes. He framed, and by his influence passed
the wharf act, every line of which showed practical
wisdom; and though a different rule of law was declared by the Court of Appeals from that which was
supposed to have prevailed in former years, yet in the
celebrated case of Stevens against the Paterson and
Newark Railroad Company, he maintained with great
learning and marked ability the opinion which he had
always held at the bar, and after he had ceased to
have any personal interest in that kind of property.
Though the riparian owner can now by making com-
pensation to the State, acquire in a full and ample
manner all the privileges of docking out into navi-
gable waters, yet so strong has been and still is the
feeling in those counties in New Jersey which border
on the sea and the great rivers, that with the excep-
tion of the Budd Tract and Black Tom's Reef, no
grant has been made in front of the shore except
to the riparian owner; and in those two cases, the
concessions have been practically rendered of no
avail, since the grants of the State have become
ultimately vested in the riparian owners. When Mr.

Zabriskie left the Senate of New Jersey, he carried with him the esteem of the people of the State.

In the year 1854, an act of the legislature of the State of New Jersey was passed, by which it was provided that the exclusive privileges commonly known as the Camden and Amboy Railroad monopoly, should expire on the 1st of January, 1869. About that time there was much discussion in the State relative to the renewal of this monopoly grant. Mr. Zabriskie at that period took strong ground against the renewal of these monopoly privileges, and at a public meeting in Jersey City, declared that the people should, with pickaxe in hand, tear up the rails, rather than have so odious a contract perpetuated. For this expression of just indignation, he was called the captain of the Pickaxe Guard. The independent portion of the community, however, sustained rather than condemned his earnest declarations, and the State of New Jersey has been relieved from the obnoxious restriction.

The practical character of Mr. Zabriskie's mind was evinced by the ability which he displayed as a railroad director, and to some extent a railroad manager.

When it became necessary for the New York and

Eric Railroad Company to make their terminus at
Jersey City, the manner in which that object should
be accomplished was of serious importance. The
finances of the company were not in the most pros-
perous condition. In 1857, commercial disasters and
bankruptcy came with their discouraging influences
upon the country. Money was to be raised, and it
required the credit of a new and distinct institution
to accomplish that object. The Long Dock charter,
which was passed February 26, 1856, was drawn by
Mr. Zabriskie. That company in name and in title
to property was distinct from the New York and Erie
Railroad Company. They had power to raise money
by issuing bonds. The tunnel was built and the line
of rails was laid from the west side of the Bergen
Hill to the Hudson. The property purchased and
filled in was ample to secure the bonds which were
issued, and the Long Dock Company being a distinct
association from the New York and Erie Railroad
Company, had a character and credit of its own, and
was not involved by the encumbrance of the several
mortgages on the main line. The plan was a success,
and the Paterson and Hudson River Railroad Company was continued to the waters of the Hudson
River through the tunnel, on the lands of the Long

Dock Company. Such is the recognized legal status of the Paterson and Hudson River Railroad Company by the Supreme Court of our State—and such was the design of Mr. Zabriskie. He was one of the most trusted advisers of Nathaniel Marsh, under whose careful, judicious and economical management, the New York and Erie Railroad Company was continued after he was appointed receiver, as the Erie Railway Company, and earned the dividends on the common and preferred stocks which were paid under his administration.

In the year 1856, Mr. Zabriskie was elected a director of the New Jersey Railroad and Transportation Company, and held that position until he was made Chancellor in the year 1866

He was not a nominal director but was placed in the important position of chairman of the executive committee of that company. He soon became master of all the affairs of the road, and gave his attention to the number of cars and locomotives which were required, the capacity of the work-shops, and the requirements of the road, and such was the accuracy of his mathematical mind, that he knew and retained in his memory the most minute details of the affairs of this corporation.

I once heard a railroad man brought up in this company say of certain plans which he suggested with reference to the working of the road, and which had received the approval of Mr. Zabriskie, that after such a sanction he did not feel much doubt of the result—such was his confidence in Mr. Zabriskie's judgment. All the duties which he performed as director of the road, were concurrent with an extensive practice in the law, in the management of cases which required learning, labor and sagacity, and in which he met as adversaries the ablest counsel of the State.

He performed the arduous duties of Chancellor with a promptness which has never been surpassed by any other officer who has held that position. No cause ever unduly hung on his hands by reason of a want of time for its examination and decision. There was an increase of business in that court during his term of office, arising out of the extension of commercial and manufacturing affairs. He held his office during a period of great progress and growth. The business of the Court of Chancery was so arranged as to give facility to suitors, and his motion days for matters of practice and injunction were an exemplification of the system which characterized the man.

His decisions show a mind positive and independent, evince labor and research, and have established for Chancellor Zabriskie an enduring fame as a judge. Though some reversals may be pointed to in the Court of Appeals, it must be remembered that he did not have the advantage of his distinguished predecessor, Chancellor Green, who, before he became Chancellor, as Chief Justice of the Supreme Court, wielding to some extent the united influence of the common law bench, exerted a controlling influence over the Court of Appeals.

Men achieve distinction or acquire wealth by the manner in which they use their time. There must be a time for labor, for rest and recreation; and the systematic distribution of time for occupation or repose becomes a matter of primary importance. When engaged in business he gave his whole attention to the matter before him. He had the power of abstracting himself from all other concerns except that which was before him. With him labor was a concentrated power and continued effort. His labors performed, he sought recreation. He attended the social entertainments given by others, and bore his part as if amusement and conversation were the sole concerns of his life. He brought others around him at the social board, and then it appeared as if hospitality was his chief pleasure. He read miscellaneous literature and found time to keep up with the knowledge of the various discoveries in science and improvement in art. He could and did give days, weeks and months to travel in his own land and European countries. The first time he went to Europe, he fixed previously the day of his departure and return, and mapped out his course of travel with most undeviating accuracy. If he designed any day to leave home and go to particular places, he fixed the time of his departure and return, and estimated with accuracy the period necessary to be occupied in the accomplishment of the object before him. Mathematical accuracy was one of the elements of his mind, and without apparent labor it seemed to be diffused over his life and controlled his conduct. To men of business he seemed to be in a most eminent degree a man of business. With those who sought to fill time by amusement as an occupation, he seemed as if his hours and days were given to similar pursuits. In his office his papers were arranged with system. His table was never encumbered by the broken piles of manuscript which is too often apt to be the case with the profession.

The chaotic confusion which mars labor and disturbs the man of business, never diverted him from the pursuit of the object before him. It was said of Mr. Grattan, the distinguished Irish orator, that he would have been far more eminent if he had only known how to use red tape to tie up his papers.

In Chancellor Zabriskie's case, there was no lumber garret, where documents and papers were piled away without system or without order.

This was one of the characteristics of Mr. Horace Binney, one of the most eminent lawyers this country has produced. He could labor with patience and system in a cause, before the stir of the impending conflict aroused him to activity. I have heard business men speak of calling on Mr. Binney. Nothing but writing materials were found on his table to indicate that he was a man of labor. The thing talked of was in many cases done on the spot, and these matters practically ended. These peculiarities of business depended largely on the structure of the mind, but they are also the result of habit enforced by the power of the will. It is said of Cyrus the Great, who established an empire that long survived his own time, that being in a mechanic's shop and observing the number of tools used, and that the master of the shop knew every tool by name, and the purpose for which it should be used, he thought it strange that a general should not know the names of all his captains, who are the instruments he must use in all his enterprises and operations. This accomplished commander following the suggestion, made himself acquainted with the names, as well as the capacity of all his captains. The genius of this great monarch and soldier was thus aided by his knowledge, which was a matter of detail in business.

Taking into consideration the combination of faculties and powers possessed by Chancellor Zabriskie, it may be said of him, that he was not surpassed at the bar of New Jersey, when he was at the noon-day of his career. He acquired a knowledge of a case with facility, though possibly not as rapid in his survey as some of his cotemporaries. His industry searched out and explored not only the most prominent points, but also the most minute details. Though somewhat involved in the presentation of a case, no point of importance which would bear on the result was omitted. His great power was to illustrate the leading principles of a cause by practical examples. He was never known to argue a cause in which he took much interest, without presenting facts and truths which appeared to be analogous, and by means · of which he impressed his hearers with a conviction of the soundness of his propositions. In the Court of Appeals, where causes were decided with rapidity, and where the judges were men widely differing in education and habits of thought, apt illustrations which appeared to cover in every particular the cause before them, produced impressions which amounted to convictions.

Talking before a jury in a simple and conversational way, with a manner which seemed full of sincerity and truth, and illustrating point after point, by some homely simile drawn from the affairs of every day life, he arrested the attention, excited the feelings whether of favor or prejudice, and secured the conviction of the twelve. While he possessed this wonderful facility of illustration, a faculty somewhat peculiar to the poetical mind, he was not what would be called a man of imagination. Nobody would ever have accused him of writing a poem, or of laying the dramatic ground-work and building the fanciful structure of a novel. If we analyze the powers of his mind, the wonder was, that while he was in so eminent a degree mathematical, with an accurate knowledge of physical laws, he should at the same time have been so fertile in illustrations and analogies to explain and enforce his meaning, a faculty which is generally supposed to be an element of the imaginative mind.

Man's faculties are oftentimes like the minerals and the metals. They run in veins, while all the immediate surroundings are common earth or barren rock. Not so with Mr. Zabriskie. He was a full man. He evinced this in every occupation or position in which he was placed. While there were some veins of greater richness than others, the ore permeated the mass. He was able as a man of business, competent to direct in affairs small or large ; he was of great learning as a lawyer; whether at nisi prius or before the bench, he had no superiors among his cotemporaries in New Jersey ; and he was able as a judge. A person who can thus in varied positions display his powers, may be called a full man.

Mr. Zabriskie was in the course of his life what our American people call a successful man. He was successful in many and varied ways. While he earned a fame which made him generally known among the people of the State and beyond our borders, he acquired property, and was looked to by men of business as eminently sagacious in the management of affairs. The good opinion of his fellow-men, in this particular was manifested by his being made a director and a trustee in so many institutions by which property and money were managed and controlled.

He was a director in railroads, in a bank, in a life insurance and trust company; a trustee of the old Jersey City Savings Bank; a director of the Jersey City Gas Company; of a turnpike company, and of other institutions by which property is managed.

In these places of trust he was not a mere nominal or silent officer. He understood well the affairs of each institution for which he was a trustee. He suggested and advised, and his voice frequently controlled the line of conduct which was pursued. He was positive in his opinions, maintaining them with firmness, and assigning reasons which frequently constrained the action of others who sat around the board in like official positions with himself. In these positions he commanded and enforced attention by his knowledge and will, rather than moved others by sympathetic influences.

Under a manner which sometimes appeared cold and repulsive, there was a warm and generous spirit. He was ready and willing to serve his friends by spending his time, his efforts and his money in their behalf.

He was a social man, and gathered around him not only persons of rank and distinction, but those for whom he felt a personal interest. When he went on the last trip of pleasure and instruction, from which he never returned, he felt that he would have little enjoyment if he went alone. He sought the companionship of one well known to him, who had been an associate in professional struggles, and toward whom he felt the regard of a genuine friendship. Thus in his last hours he received that kind attention, that genuine sympathy, due only to those who are good and true, and which are among the highest tributes which mortals can bestow on each other.

He had passed through a life of labor, usefulness, distinction and honor. He had seen the peoples of the old world, and observed closely the operations of their institutions and laws. He had acquired a competency. He had retired from the highest judicial position of his State. He sought a more intimate knowledge of that vast continent, over a large portion of which, in his own time, he had seen the power and political institutions of his native country extended. He passed the Rocky Mountains and viewed that vast and varied domain, with all its beauty and grandeur, which stretches to the setting sun. Impressed with glories of the most sublime natural scenery, having witnessed the unparalleled progress of a great State, the offspring of our glorious Union, glittering with the rich robes and jewels of a younger sister, upon the shores of the Pacific ocean, he sought to return to his home there to celebrate with his family and his friends the anniversary of that Declaration of Independence which gave birth to an empire, and to take his part among that body of men, who had been selected to frame anew a charter for a constitutional government.

From such scenes and under such circumstances, he was called to that rest which belongs to the faithful and the true.

CORRESPONDENCE.

———— ✦ — ——

JERSEY CITY, JANUARY 3, 1874.

REV. W. H. CAMPBELL, L. L. D.:

Dear Sir—The friends of the late Chancellor Zabriskie are about to publish a memorial book or pamphlet to perpetuate his memory, containing the eulogy pronounced by the Hon. I. W. Scudder, &c.

It would afford us much pleasure to be able to publish your sermon, pronounced upon the occasion of his funeral.

If you can furnish us with a copy for publication, you will greatly oblige, and I remain,

Very truly, yours,

JACOB WEART,
Chairman of Committee.

NEW BRUNSWICK, JANUARY 12, 1874.

J. WEART, ESQ., CHAIRMAN, &c.:

Dear Sir—I have received your note requesting for publication a copy of the address delivered at the funeral of Hon. A. O. Zabriskie. I send it to you with pleasure, mingled with great sorrow at the loss of so dear a friend.

With great respect,

Yours, very truly,

W. H. CAMPBELL.

SERMON BY DR. CAMPBELL.

Here lies your dead friend, and here seated around his body are the living friends, who mourn his departure and are about to bear him hence for burial. And here, as is right, the ambassador of Christ is called on to speak to the living words befitting this occasion, and to speak of the dead those truthful words, which may instruct, comfort, strengthen and warn the living. And what shall be said to the living? Those words of our Saviour are the most timely to-day:

"Watch therefore; for ye know not what hour your Lord doth come."—Matt. xxiv., 42.

In these words the Master speaks *of himself*, and he speaks *to you*. He, who has come and taken away your friend, tells you to watch, because he is coming for you, and coming too without giving you any warning as to the time of his approach. And as every one of these words is weighty, let us weigh them well.

It is *your Lord* who here speaks, and who is coming for you. Jesus of Nazareth, who lived on earth as a man of sorrows, and died as a malefactor on the cross, is your Lord.

Lord. His was a twofold nature. He was a true man in body and soul, that he might obey and suffer as a substitute for sinful men. He also became man to show the possibilities of human nature, when divine power had undertaken to raise it from its degradation. But he was God also, the eternal and only begotten Son of God. As such he thought it not robbery to be equal with God, though he had emptied himself of his glory, and made himself of no reputation, that he might do good to men. But as the Son of God he also holds and does the duties of a divine office, as the *Word of God.* As such the Son is the Spokesman of Deity, and every revelation of himself, which God has ever made to men, has been effected through the Son in his office of the eternal Word.

1. Thus it was he who spoke this world into being. "All things were made by him; and without him was not anything made that was made." And while "the heavens declare the glory of God, and the firmament showeth his handy work," all this revelation of the wisdom, power and goodness of God, as seen in the visible creation, is made by the eternal Son, the Word, the Spokesman of God.

2. By him too "all things consist," "upholding all

things by the word of his power." We speak of the physical laws by which the material world is kept in being, but we mean thereby that fixed and uniform course, whereby the Son of God holds in being the world he has created, and by which sustenance he, as the Word, makes a constant revelation of the wisdom, power and goodness of God. There was then a depth of meaning in the Psalmist's words: "Day unto day uttereth speech, and night unto night showeth knowledge. There is no speech nor language where their voice is not heard." That voice is the utterance of the divine Spokesman, making known with a ceaseless reiteration the glory of God. This daily upholding and governing of the physical world is giving evermore a new revelation of the wisdom, power and goodness of God.

3. So also the Word has done and is doing his work of revealing God, by setting up and continuing a moral government in the world.

It is necessary in order to have a moral government among men, that the subjects of it should be capable of knowing *the just, the good and the true,* and feeling the duty, beauty and desirableness of having justice, goodness and truth as the characteristics of oneself. Now conscience in man fits him to be thus a subject of moral government, and the Word has placed it in the human breast to be man's monitor and guide. Furthermore he has established here that fixed order of sequences, whereby rewards and punishments are visited upon men according to their deeds. And the Word speaks both in conscience and this fixed order. That voice is ever audible. It says, it shall be well with him who heeds the law of God, and it shall be ill with him who breaks its precepts. And it is the voice of the eternal Word who thus reveals the justice of God.

4. And now when, in utter disregard of God speaking by conscience and the dispensation of rewards and punishments, man had trodden under foot the justice, goodness and truth of God, the Word comes to make his fourth revelation, transcending all others, the revelation of mercy, *God pities sinners.* He continues inflexibly just, and yet becomes a Saviour. These two attributes, which appear to be so diametrically opposed to each other, are to be manifested in God, both in him in an infinite degree, and yet both in perfect harmony. Justice demands and must have full satisfaction for all the transgressions of the law, while infinite mercy demands and must have the full, free pardon of the transgressor. This revelation of

something hereafter to be accomplished the Word announced in Eden, when man began to sin. And ever after down along the track of time he spoke, unfolding little by little but ever more fully the wondrous story of the blended justice and mercy of God. At length the fullness of time having come, the full revelation burst at once upon the view of angels and men, when the incarnate Son of God was seen nailed to the cross, the substitute of sinners, and bearing for them the wrath of God. Thus the divine justice was fully satisfied, and thus the way was opened up for the mercy and love of God to be poured out upon sinners.

Now then it is fully revealed. Man can become once more a son of God through the obedience and sufferings of Jesus the Mediator. He becomes too a son in expectancy of an inheritance. A home awaits him in the Father's house, and he is here preparing for it. The mansion in heaven is being made ready for him, and he on earth is being made ready for it. And in this preparation the fourth revelation of the Word has wondrous efficacy. What power is there in the teaching and life of Christ to free a man from the dominion of sin as well as from its guilt, when the Holy Spirit applies to the soul the truth that there is in that life and teaching. Wonderful life, so just, so pure, so tender, so kind, so unselfish, so self-sacrificing, so unwearied in goodness, so perfect, infinite in its mercy for sinners. It was indeed a revelation of God. And when the Holy Spirit opens a man's heart to see its beauty, and creates his heart anew so that he can feel that beauty, and love God and Christ because of it, it works wonders in the human soul. It transforms it into the divine image. It makes man a partaker of the divine nature. It begins in the soul a holiness like that of God, causing a joy in thinking of God and becoming like him, which is a foretaste of heaven as well as a preparation for it. Oh, this wonderful fourth revelation of the Son of God. What it has done for men! What it is now doing! What it shall hereafter do for them! Blessed is he unto whom the Lord has thus come in the power of his fourth revelation.

5. But the next revelation which the Word makes unto men, is when he comes as the Lord to take them away into the world of spirits. Then the unseen world, of which we now have knowledge by revelation alone, will be seen and known by consciousness. Then the connection between the present and the future, between the life here and the life after the

death of the body, will be made clear. And it will be seen that the present is the preparation for the future life—that keeping the heart here is most important, since out of the kept heart alone are the issues of life—that he who sows to the flesh shall of the flesh reap corruption, while he alone who sows to the Spirit shall of the Spirit reap life everlasting.

This fifth revelation the Son of God, the Word, has now made to your deceased friend. And soon it will be made to you. *When*, no one knows but the Revealer, your Lord. And therefore he gives you this exhortation, *watch*. That is, be prepared for my coming for you by believing on me as the sacrifice for your sins, and as the source of grace by which you shall be prepared to dwell in my father's house above. Oh, what a revelation that new state of existence after death will be! That state, as the Word shall make it known to each disembodied spirit by the ministry of angels, will be a revelation of unspeakable joy or of unutterable anguish, according as each has accepted or rejected the gracious invitations of Jesus Christ. All day long through the whole of the earthly life the voice of mercy calls on men to flee from wrath and to cast themselves upon the care of him who is mighty to save. All, who do so, will have on dying a wondrous revelation of love and blessedness, when the enthroned King will own *them* before the angels, who owned him among men. And they will then know as never before what sorrow is, who, having despised the voice of mercy on earth, have naught to expect at death but the revelation of wrath.

6. The last revelation of God to men, will be made by the Son of God, as all the others have been. This is to be made at the general judgment, which is to be conducted by Christ. "Because he hath appointed a day, in the which he will judge the world in righteousness by that man whom he hath ordained; whereof he hath given assurance unto all men, in that he hath raised him from the dead."

There is a peculiar fitness in the committing of the final judgment of the world to the Word. For since he everywhere else has spoken for God unto men, so here he speaks, making the last and fullest revelation. Then all the dark problems of earth will be solved; its wrongs be made right, and all the ways of God to men be justified in the vindication of everything that is just, true and good, and in the condemnation of all that is unjust, false and evil. And in that last judgment the glory of Christ will be plainly manifested.

By his godhead he will know all hearts and all actions. He will need none to help him in deciding each case at once and with perfect justice. And there will not be one in that vast assembly, countless to men or angels, who will have a word to say against his sentence, however heavily it may bear down upon the soul.

The revelations at death and the judgment will be in accordance with the life here on earth. As one watches or neglects watching will there be hereafter joy or woe. And to watch is to heed all the four revelations of Christ, which have been already received. Especially must one heed the revelation of mercy, as made known in the gospel and displayed at Calvary. Get near the cross to gaze not only upon the dying lamb of God, who taketh away the sins of the world, but to have his precious blood drop upon you, sprinkle and save you. Say, as you dwell ever watchfully near it:

> " Nothing in my hand I bring,
> Simply to thy cross I cling ;
> Naked come to thee for dress,
> Helpless look to thee for grace ;
> Foul I to the fountain fly,
> Wash me, Saviour, or I die."

Be thus prepared for these awful future revelations.

And now I am to speak of the dead. Nor is the task difficult or irksome. It is both easy and pleasant. *Easy* because the character had strongly marked features. It was, too, quite symmetrical. It had in it no contradictions, no politic concealments, none of the crookednesses, which spring from the hypocrisies of selfishness. Mr. Zabriskie's character was an epistle written in plain, legible letters, and it could be read and known by all men. It is also a *pleasant* and not an irksome task, say rather a privilege to describe this character. For it was a good character. One can dwell upon it with great satisfaction, mingled only with the regret, that he, who bore it, will be seen no more here.

Everything about Mr. Zabriskie's mind was massive like his body. He had a great intellect. He was the first in his class at school, first in his class at college, first as a student of law, first as a lawyer at the bar, and first as a judge upon the bench. A distinguished lawyer, whose opinions have great weight with you all, told me that A. O. Zabriskie was a lawyer, whom he always feared to have as his opposing counsel, because he was never sure before hand what his line of argument was going to be. And this remark of the brother lawyer touches the very point of Mr. Z.'s intellectual character. He was a genius. He could discern the new, where there was the new to be discovered, and he could use it with all the powers of a mind, that was well betokened by his strong arm, which moved up and down, and back and forth most enerjetically, as he gave forth his weighty arguments. At the same time so well-balanced an intellect had he, that no inventive powers could lead him to disregard *authority*, which ought to and must have so much weight in the law. And this regard for authority made him a diligent student in many departments of knowledge. He was well-read not only in law, but also in history, the natural sciences, anatomy, medicine and theology. And especially as any of these bore upon his own profession. And accuracy also marked him in every department of his studies. What he had studied at all, was thoroughly studied.

He had also a great soul. By this I mean that he had large and strong affections. He had a large heart in his large body. Some men's affections are strong, but their exercise is limited to kindred. Mr. Z. loved his relatives dearly, but his regards, sympathies and deeds of love extended far beyond the circle of his kindred. He was very undemonstrative as to what he felt and did in the way of kindness and beneficence. Much of what he did has become known by the information of the benefitted. Nor did he weary of doing kindnesses, when he was treated ungratefully. Once when so treated a friend said to him, "I suppose you have learned a lesson, which will keep you from ever doing a like deed." His reply was: "I would do it again under like circumstances; for the needs of society require just such acts." Could the two last letters which Mr. Z. wrote (bearing date a few days before his death and addressed to persons not his blood-relatives) be read to this assembly, none here would need further proof of the largeness of his heart.

He was also a conscientious man. He took pains to know his duty, and when known he faithfully discharged it. As a boy, he was mirthful, full of fun, and even of harmless mischief. When he became a man, boyish fun gave place to cheerful manliness. And yet boyhood, manhood, middle life and riper years displayed a character without a blot. He has gone in and out among you at Millstone, Princeton, Newark, Hackensack and Jersey City, and bear witness, fellow-citizens, whom of you has he ever injured? Or who of you can accuse him of aught evil?

And now as to the greatest interest of all, was he watching when his Lord came?

On this point I have several remarks to make. Mr. Z. was a firm believer in the doctrines of the Reformed Church, in which he was born, baptized, reared and spent his life. And he was a firm believer of these three vital truths of Christianity:

1. The Bible is the infallible word of God, given to teach men the way of salvation.

2. Man is a sinner, and can only be saved by faith in the atonement of Christ the eternal and only begotten Son of God.

3. The work of the Holy Spirit is necessary for the enlightenment, renewal and sanctification of the heart. Except a man be born again he cannot see the Kingdom of God.

In view of this belief and of his upright, consistent life, he was urged again and again to make a public profession of his belief and purpose of life to obey Christ. Had he applied to the Church, he would have been received at once. Now why did he not thus publicly profess? In my judgment he was in a large measure deterred by a wrong view of the third article of his belief, the necessity of the regenerating work of the Holy Spirit. He was waiting for some almost miraculous manifestation of the presence and power of the Spirit, which would put his Christian experience quite out of the domain of faith, and make it a matter of sight. He failed to see, that the power of the Spirit is exercised in silence and unseen, and is known only by its effects—that religion is not a miracle but a life—that he who walks lovingly and obediently in the path which the Spirit points out in the Scriptures is led by the Spirit and is a son of God.

Mr. Z. was waiting for something which never came, and never would have come, if he had lived on to the end of the century. And yet the Spirit may have been with him all the time, though he knew it not. As he read the Scriptures day by day, as was his wont; and as he looked up to God for guidance, and committed his way unto him; who are you and I to exclude him from the divine favor, because he did not commune? When we, notwithstanding our frequent communions, may at last be castaways. And just here comes in the lesson of warning to the living. Sinful, helpless, cast yourselves on the divine mercy, and do it in the divine way. One can never get on earth so near to Christ

as at the Supper of the Lord.   The language of such
an approach is:

> " Just as I am—without one plea,
>   But that thy blood was shed for me,
>   And that thou bidst me come to thee.
>
>   Just as I am—Thy love unknown
>   Has broken every barrier down,
>   Now to be thine, yea thine alone,
>   O, Lamb of God, I come ! I come ! "

This plea, excluding all else but Christ, moves
heaven to do that, which heaven will never reverse.

PROCEEDINGS IN THE COURT OF ERRORS AND APPEALS
AT TRENTON.

[Report taken from the *True American*.]

Attorney-General Gilchrist called the attention of the Court
to the death of the late Chancellor. He said :

May it please your Honors : On Friday afternoon last, the
family of the late Chancellor Zabriskie received information
by telegram, dated at Truckee, California, from Mr. Knapp,
a member of the bar, that Chancellor Zabriskie was very ill.
At ten o'clock on the evening of the same day, they received
a telegram that he was dead. No particulars of his death
have been received, except that he died of erysipelas, and
from the fact that the two dispatches were from Truckee, and
several hours apart, it is concluded that the Chancellor did
not die in the cars. News of his illness excited the sympathy
of his neighbors. News of his death startled the whole State,
for he was widely and generally known, respected and loved.
The death of so distinguished a man, so lately a member of
this court, seems to justify a departure from the general rule
that the court do not place upon its records a memorial of the
death of any but those who are members of the court, but it
is the duty of the living to bury the dead, and, though it is
no part of the duty of the living to praise them, yet when so
distinguished a man falls, under circumstances so peculiar as
those which attended the death of Chancellor Zabriskie, a

death so sudden, while on a journey of intelligent observation
and recreation in a distant State, we must mourn our loss. It
assuages a grief that we feel to dwell upon his virtues ; and
if it be praise to speak of them, it is nature that speaks.
What was weak and mortal in him we find remaining in our-
selves. What was good in him we have lost. We cannot
but mourn the loss of these. Mr. Gilchrist continued, at
some length, to extol the character of the Chancellor as a man,
a lawyer and a judge; and among other things, said that
even his errors and defects showed the greatness of his soul.
He remarked upon the simplicity, modesty and gentleness of
the Chancellor in social intercourse and even amid the under
contracts of professional life, and held up the Chancellor's
intellectual, moral and social character as one to be emulated
and imitated, remarking that from it not only the bar but the
bench could learn many lessons. During Mr. Gilchrist's remarks he developed the following facts: Deceased was born
at Greenbush, opposite Albany, N. Y., on June 10th, 1807,
and was taken to Millstone, N. J., in 1811. He was entered
at Princeton College in 1823, and graduated at Princeton in
1825. He commenced to study law in 1825, with James S.
Green, Esq., of Princeton, and was admitted to practice in
November, 1828. He was admitted a counsellor in 1831, and
settled first at Newark. In 1830 he removed to Hackensack,
and there remained in practice until 1849. While in Hackensack he held the office of Surrogate and Prosecutor of Pleas.
He became Chancellor on the 1st of May, 1866, served his
term and died of erysipelas at Truckee, Cal., June 27th, 1873.
The Attorney-General concluded by moving the court, that

out of respect to the memory of so great a jurist and man the court do now adjourn.

Chancellor Runyon replied :

The news of the death of the distinguished jurist, whose demise has been so eloquently and feelingly announced to the court by the Attorney-General, was received with the deepest regret. Having just retired from a position he had filled with great honor to himself and his State, having rounded up a life of usefulness, full of years and full of honors; having well served his generation, he has fallen asleep. His long connection with this court as its presiding officer; his long and intimate connection with its business before he came to its bench ; his identification with the administration of justice as lawyer and judge, for nearly half a century, render eulogium unnecessary among those with whom he has been associated. His name is added to those of whose record New Jersey is proud. Much as she prizes her history and its associations, the valor and patriotism of her sons on field and deck, proud as she is of the character of her people, of her resources and the enterprise of her citizens, she reckons among her brightest jewels the lives of such as he; the men who have given her her great character for justice, for law and order. To speak their names would be to utter the household words of her firesides. The deceased was a consummate lawyer, a just, patient and impartial judge ; a citizen always on the side of the right as God gave him to see the right ; conservative in his views, firm and positive in his convictions, an honor to the State and the nation. When he left us his eye was not dim nor his natural force abated; he looked forward, as well he might, to future useful labor for the State, after that vacation which he intended should be but for a few days, but which God, in His providence, has made eternal. His life was full of high and honorable example, of duty conscientiously discharged and life's labor well and diligently done.

The Attorney-General's motion was adopted.

RESOLUTIONS ADOPTED BY THE CONSTITUTIONAL COMMIS-
SION OF THE STATE OF NEW JERSEY, JULY 8TH, 1873,
ON THE DEATH OF HON. ABRAHAM O. ZABRISKIE.

While reverently bowing to the dispensation of an all-wise
providence, which has called from the sphere of his earthly
influence, in the full vigor and maturity of his great powers,
the late President of this body, the Honorable A. O. Zabriskie, a due respect to the memory of a great life ended, sanc-
tions the expression of our sorrow at the irreparable loss this
body has sustained in his death.

Honored by the State and his fellow-citizens with high
trusts, he always merited the confidence reposed in him, by
the faithful and conscientious discharge of every duty ; as a
citizen he was patriotic and public spirited; as a lawyer,
learned, ingenious and faithful ; as an advocate, fearless, zealous and powerful ; as a jurist, able, just and upright ; as a
legislator, while he tenaciously maintained and upheld all that
had been proved to be beneficial, he was willing and eager to
correct such portions of the law as experience had demon-
strated to be erroneous, and to eradicate provisions which
lapse of time had rendered obsolete.

Resolved, That this Commission, charged by the Legislative
and Executive branches of the Government with the respons-
ible duty of suggesting amendments to the organic laws of.
the State, has by his death been deprived not only of its
President, but of its most valued adviser. Massive in intel-

L. of C.

lect, rich in culture, varied in experience, wise in counsel, noble in impulse, untiring in industry, exhaustive in research, he was pre-eminently fitted properly and satisfactorily to discharge the arduous duties with which he as a member was entrusted.

Resolved, That we deeply sympathize with the family of the deceased, and that a copy of these resolutions, properly engrossed, be transmitted to them by the President and enrolled on the minutes of the Commission.

PROCEEDINGS AT THE BOARD OF CHOSEN FREEHOLDERS OF
HUDSON COUNTY, AT THEIR MEETING, JULY 3D, 1873.

Freeholder Van Nostrand announced the death of the late
Chancellor Zabriskie to the Board, and moved that the Counsel of the Board prepare a suitable set of resolutions to be
presented to the Board.

Counsel Jacob Weart, Esq., reported the following resolutions concerning the death of Hon. A. O. Zabriskie, which
were read and adopted unanimously, as follows :

WHEREAS, It has pleased God to call from our midst by
death the Hon. Abraham O. Zabriskie, late Chancellor of the
State of New Jersey, and also late the Cousel of this Board,
and humbly submitting to the dispensation of divine providence ; it is hereby

Resolved, That we, the members of the Board of Chosen
Freeholders of the County of Hudson, do deeply mourn the
loss of the late Chancellor, the Hon. Abraham O. Zabriskie,
who has been suddenly stricken down by death, in a distant
State, far away upon the slopes of the Pacific.

Resolved, That it is due that we express our feelings of
respect for the many wise and able opinions rendered upon
various matters to this Board, during the several years while
he was its legal advisor; and that his legal opinions, on file
with the Clerk of this Board, will be lasting monuments to
his great legal ability.

Resolved, That in the capacity of senator from this county, he did honor to us, great service to the State, and that his senatorial term will ever be held in the highest estimation by the people of this county.

Resolved, That in the office of Chancellor he wore the judicial ermine with great lustre. Of untiring energy, great industry, and a profound knowledge of the law, he brought to the office every requisite which made him eminently useful to the State; and his reported legal opinions will be read and respected wherever the law is faithfully administered, and equity jurisprudence is revered and esteemed.

Resolved, That we regard as the crowning act of his life, the exercise of his influence as a private citizen, and his great efforts to prevent the extension of the monopoly privileges of railroads, a measure which was defeated a few years since, mainly by his voice and personal exertion.

Resolved, That we do deeply feel our loss as citizens, as neighbors, and friends, as the departed filled up a full measure of usefulness in all the Christian walks of life.

Resolved, That the clerk of the Board forward a copy of these resolutions to the family of the deceased, and that they be entered upon our minutes, and that we do attend his funeral.

www.ingramcontent.com/pod-product-compliance
Lightning Source LLC
Chambersburg PA
CBHW022140090426
42742CB00010B/1336